Air Power

F-22 RAPTOR

MEGAN COOLEY PETERSON

BLACK RABBIT BOOKS

Bolt is published by Black Rabbit Books
P.O. Box 3263, Mankato, Minnesota, 56002.
www.blackrabbitbooks.com

Jennifer Besel, editor; Grant Gould & Michael Sellner, designers; Omay Ayres, photo researcher

Library of Congress Cataloging-in-Publication Data
Names: Peterson, Megan Cooley, author.
Title: F-22 Raptor / by Megan Cooley Peterson.
Description: Mankato, Minnesota : Black Rabbit Books, 2019. | Series: Bolt. Air power | Includes bibliographical references and index. | Audience: Age: 9-12. | Audience: Grade: 4 to 6.
Identifiers: LCCN 2017024395 (print) | LCCN 2017026162 (ebook) | ISBN 9781680724998 (ebook) | ISBN 9781680723830 (library binding) | ISBN 9781680726770 (paperback)
Subjects: LCSH: F-22 (Jet fighter plane)—Juvenile literature.
Classification: LCC UG1242.F5 (ebook) | LCC UG1242.F5 P473 2019 (print) | DDC 358.4/383—dc23
LC record available at https://lccn.loc.gov/2017024395

Printed in China. 3/18

Image Credits

af.mil: US Air Force, 3, 25, 27; US Air Force/Ken Chandler, 6–7, 16–17; US Air Force/Master Sgt. Andy Dunaway, 22; Alamy: andrew chittock, 9 (t); Rodolfo Arpia, 13 (t); Stephen Lake, 12 (t); US Air Force Photo, 4–5, 9 (b), 13 (b); allwallpapers.info: 26 (r), 31; commons.wikimedia.org: 12 (b); defense.gov: US Department of Defense, 28–29; en.wikipedia.org: US Air Force, Cover, 10 (bl), 18–19; hill.af.mil: US Air Force, 26 (l); iStock: hh5800, 12–13 (bkgd); mjf795, 32; sdelanounas.ru: 15 (t); Shutterstock: Darryl Brooks, 10 (tl); DmitriyRazinkov, 15 (b); Everett Historical, 1; inspired-fiona, 20 (bkgd); www.the-blueprints.com: 10–11, 20–21
Every effort has been made to contact copyright holders for material reproduced in this book. Any omissions will be rectified in subsequent printings if notice is given to the publisher.

CONTENTS

CHAPTER 1

PROTECTING the Skies

An F-22 Raptor fighter jet soared over the Persian Gulf. Its mission—guard a **drone** watching the area. Suddenly, two enemy fighter jets began moving toward the drone.

Scared Them Away

The F-22 snuck up on the enemies. The pilot flew right under one plane. The enemies had no idea the F-22 was there. Then the pilot flew near one enemy's wing. When they spotted the F-22, they quickly sped away. They knew they couldn't beat the F-22 in a fight.

CHAPTER 2

HISTORY of the F-22 Raptor

Before the F-22, the U.S. military used the F-15. The F-15 fighter can't hide from **radar**. The military needed a fighter that could. The government held a competition to design a new jet.

F-22 Raptor vs. F-15 Eagle

F-22 Raptor		F-15 Eagle
1	crew	1 or 2
more than 1,840 miles (2,961 kilometers)	range	more than 3,450 miles (5,552 km)
2	engines	2

F-22 Weapons

cannon

fires 100 rounds per second

2 center weapons bays

hold radar-guided missiles

2 side weapons bays

hold heat-seeking missiles

A New Sneaky, Fast Jet

The new jet had to have **stealth**. And it had to be fast. Two teams created designs for a new jet. The team led by the Lockheed Martin company won the competition.

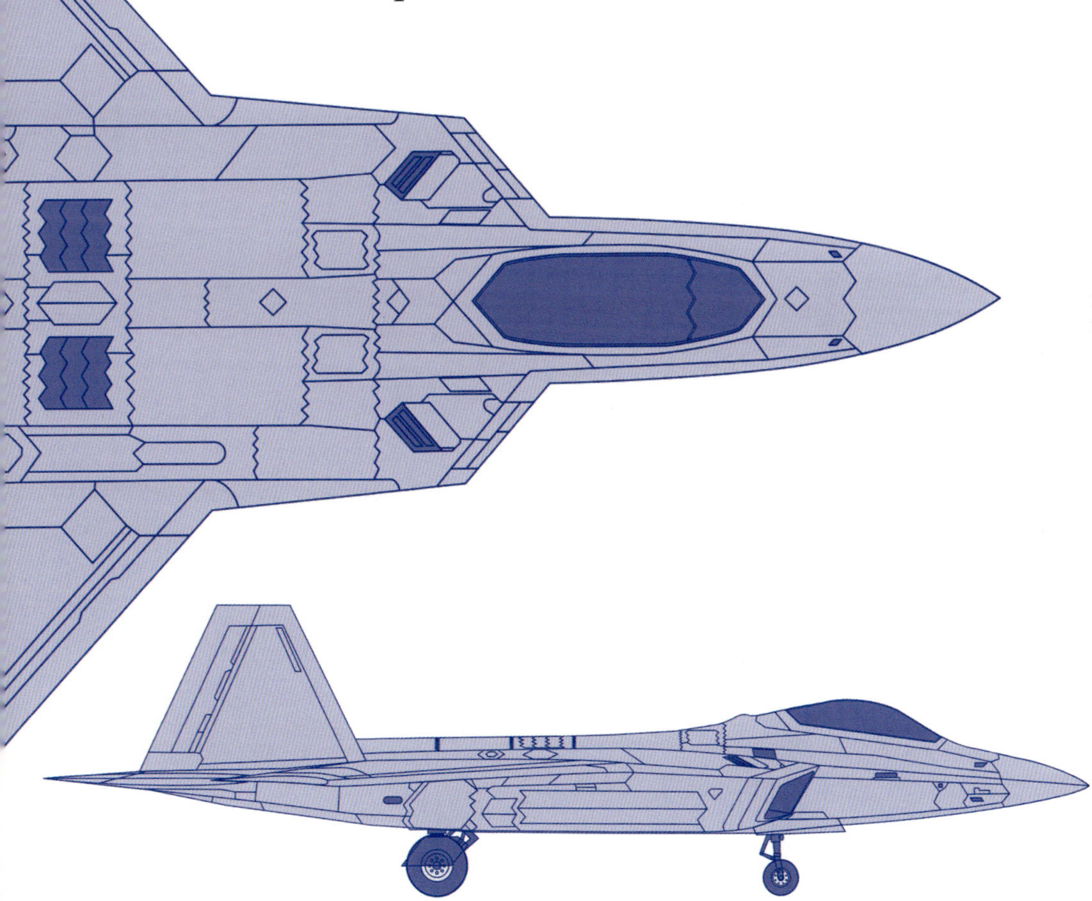

F-22 RAPTOR TIMELINE

April 1997
first public showing

September 1997
first flight

1990

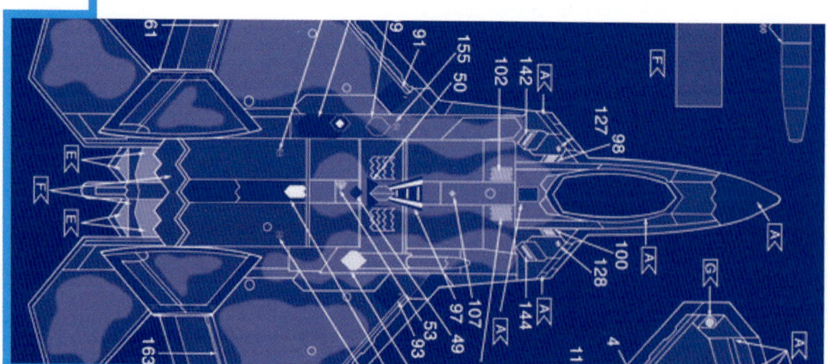

1991
Lockheed's team wins government contract.

2005

Plane is ready for missions.

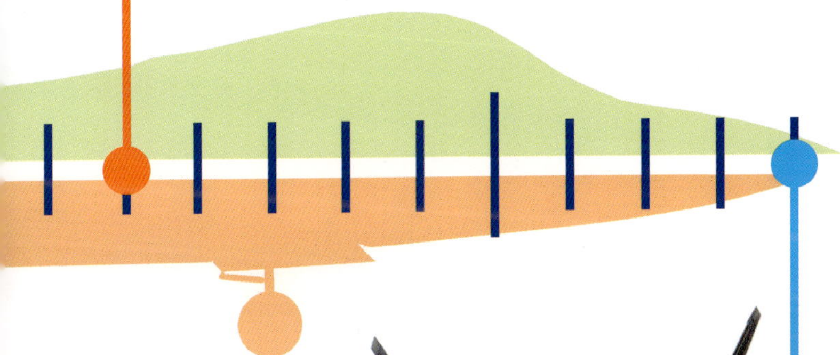

2014

first combat mission

CHAPTER 3

F-22 Raptor FEATURES

The F-22 is made for secrecy. A coating on the plane soaks in radar signals. This feature lets the plane fly without being seen on radar. Other pilots don't see the F-22 until it's too late.

The F-22 is the size of a bumblebee on radar.

F-22 RAPTOR PARTS

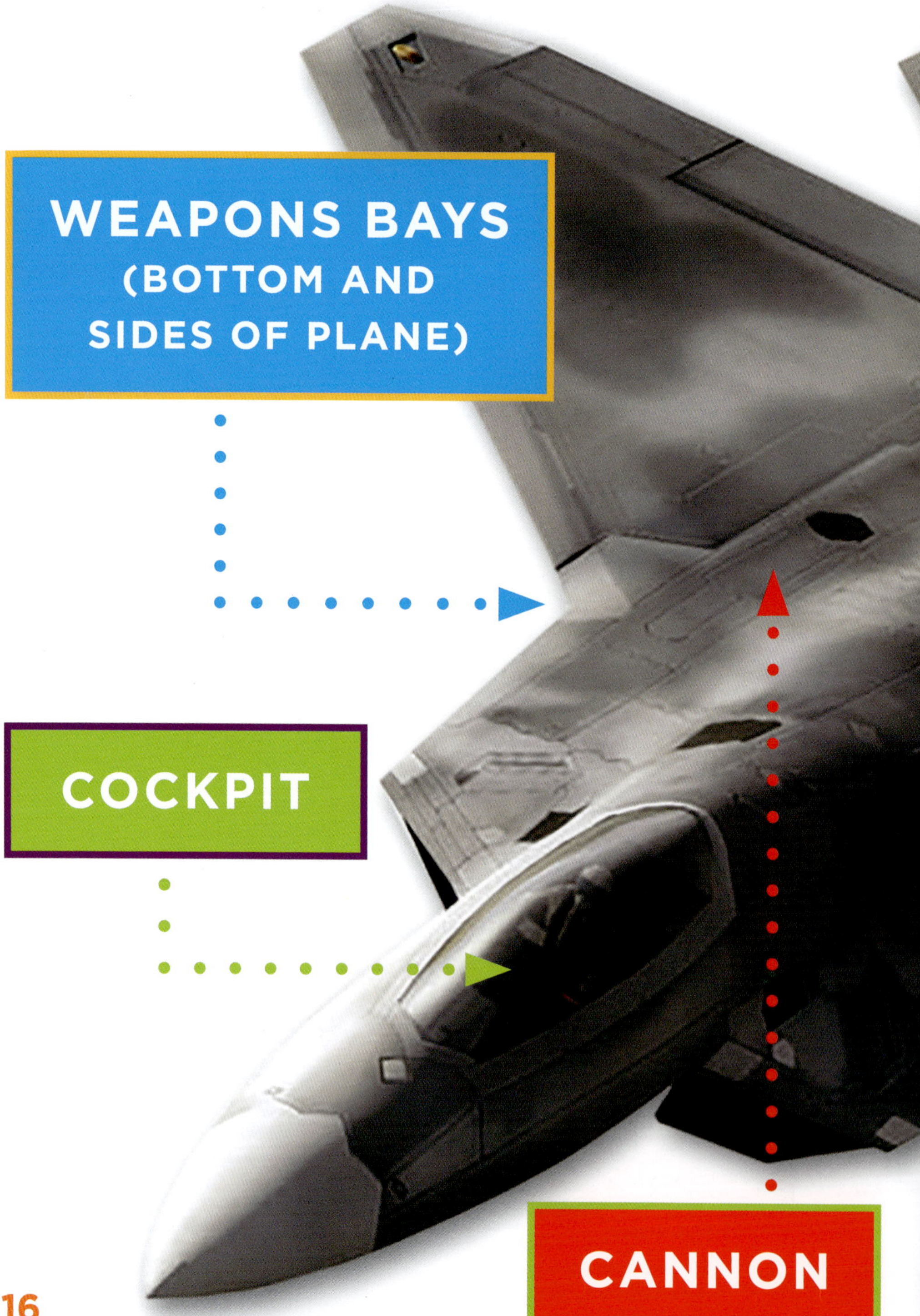

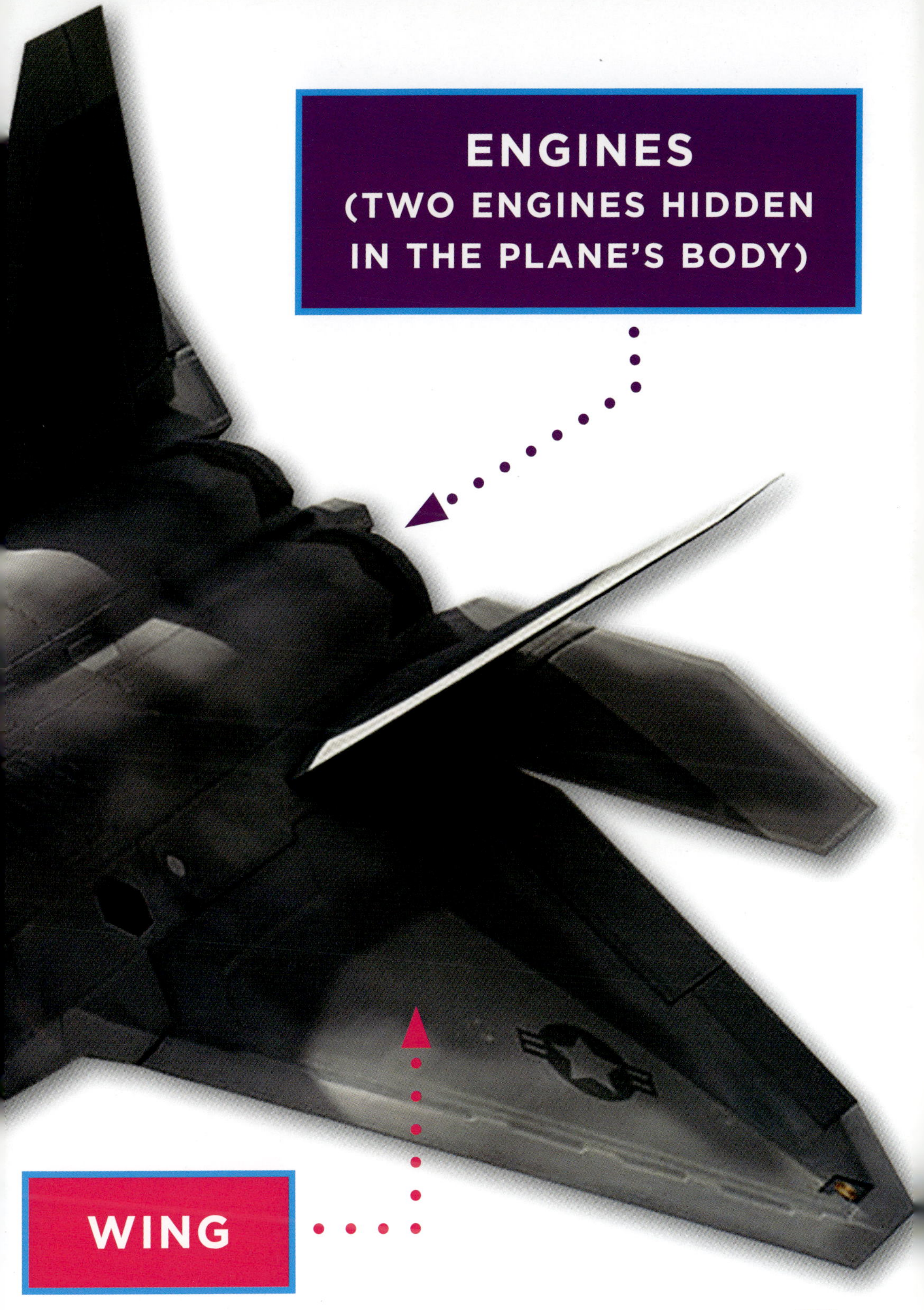
ENGINES (TWO ENGINES HIDDEN IN THE PLANE'S BODY)
WING

A New Kind of Fast

Most fighters use **afterburners** to go **supersonic**. Afterburners give a plane more thrust. But they use a lot of fuel.

F-22s fly supersonic for long periods of time. They do it without afterburners.

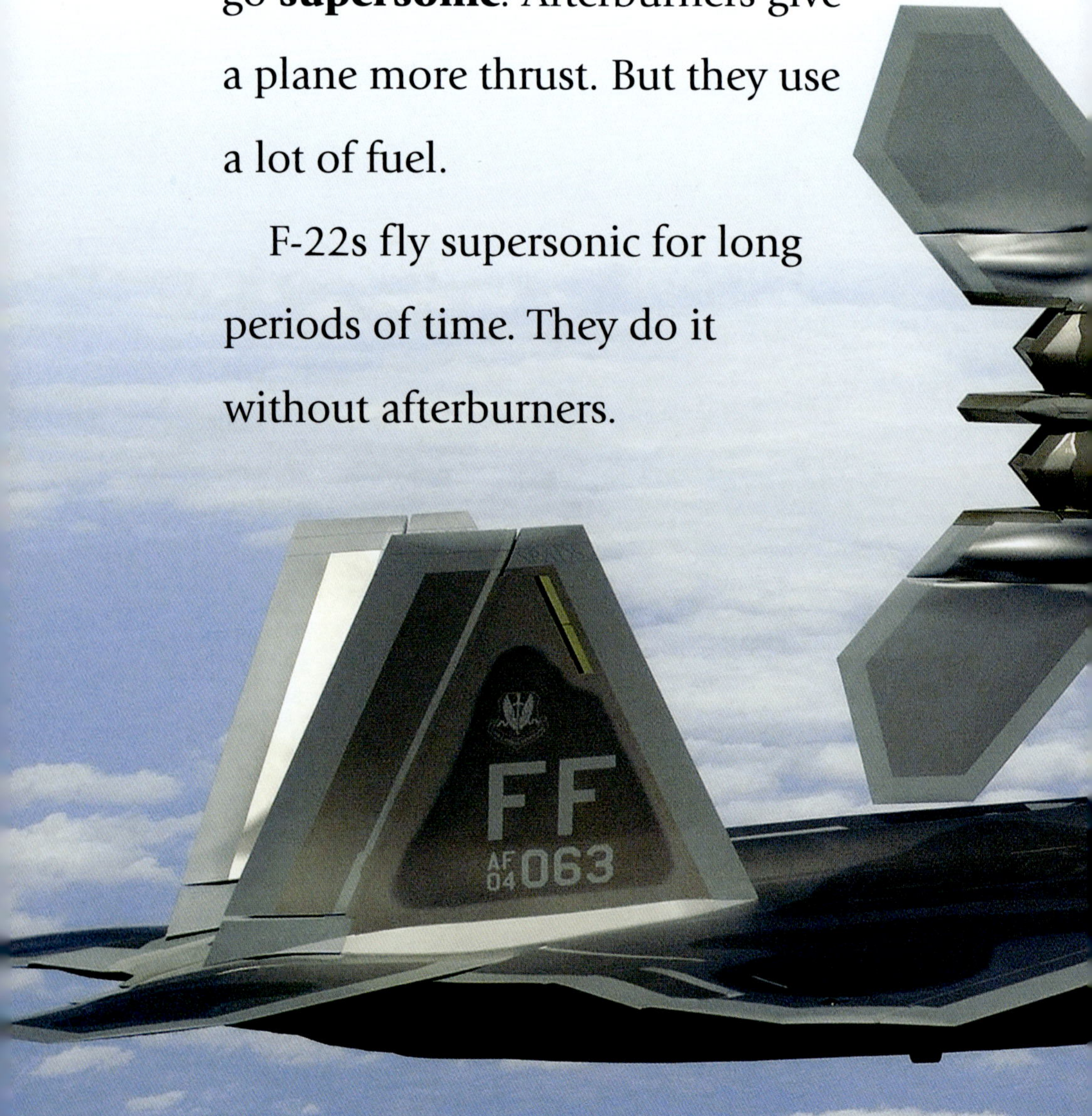

F-22s fly up to about 1,500 miles (2,414 km) per hour.

F-22 RAPTOR STATS

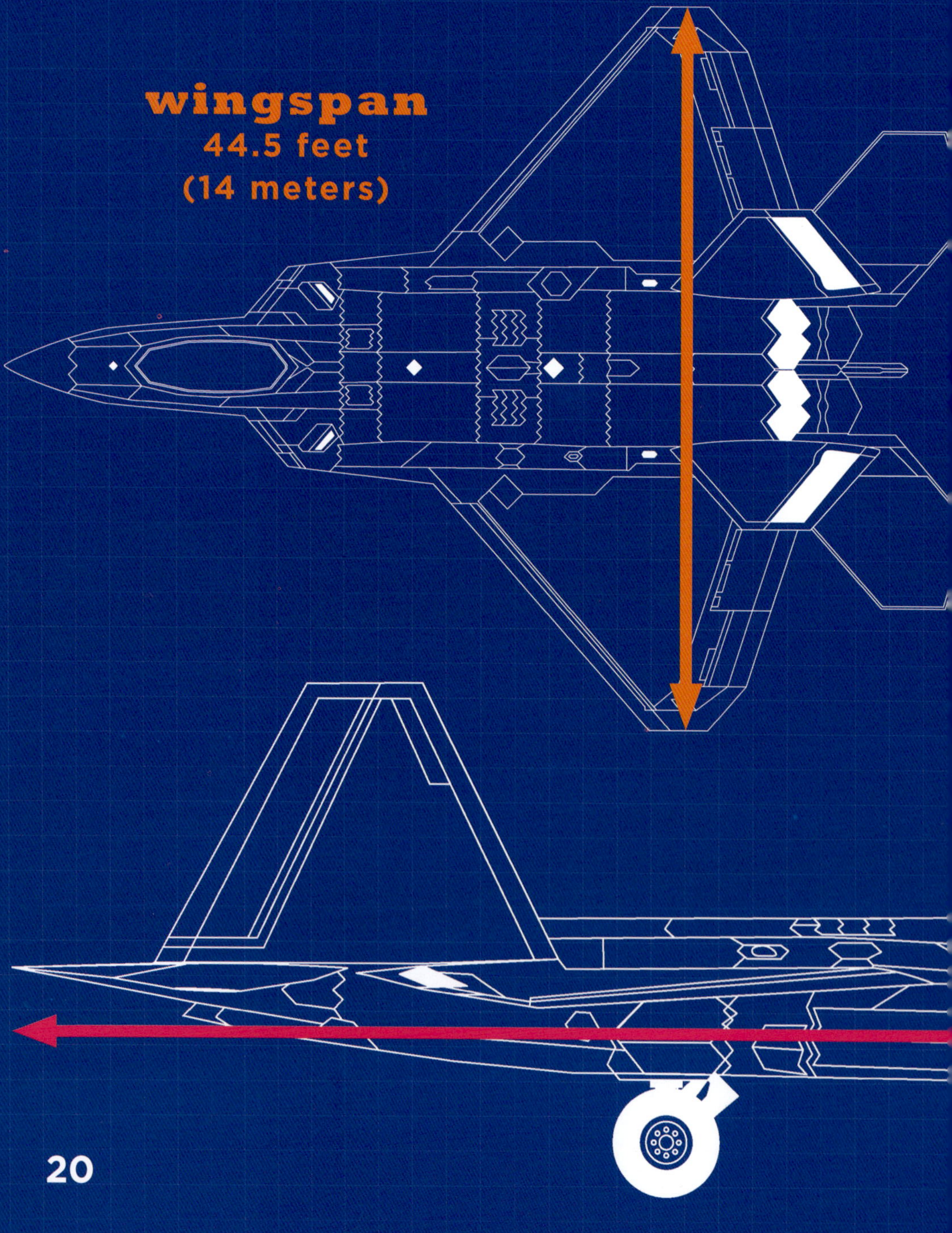

Quick Turns

The F-22 isn't just faster than most jets. It also handles better. Its frame is made of titanium. This material keeps the plane light. F-22s make turns that would damage other jets.

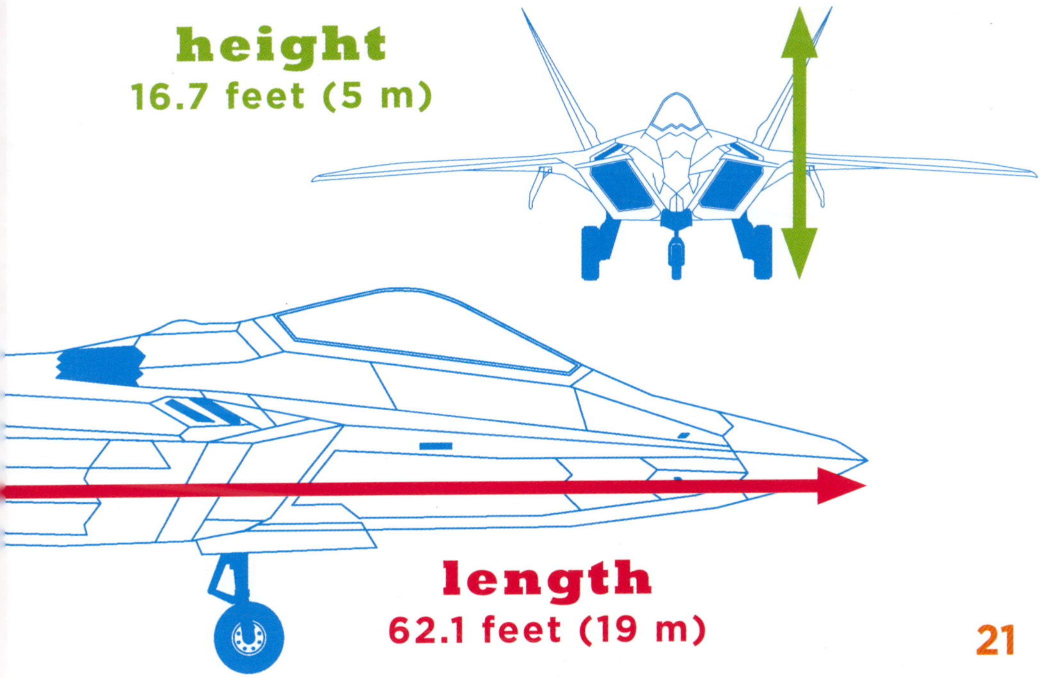

CHAPTER 4

The F-22 Raptor in ACTION

The F-22's main job is to shoot down enemy planes. The Raptor is hard to beat in a **dogfight**.

F-22s also destroy ground targets. They flew their first mission in 2014. They bombed a **terrorist** building.

Scary to See

Just the sight of an F-22 scares most enemies. In August 2016, F-22s flew over the country of Syria. Two enemy fighters spotted them. The enemies quickly flew away.

BY THE NUMBERS

NUMBER OF F-22s IN THE U.S. AIR FORCE (as of 2017)

83,500 POUNDS
(37,875 kilograms)
MAXIMUM TAKEOFF WEIGHT
MORE THAN 50,000 FEET (15,240 m)
HOW HIGH THE F-22 CAN FLY

Powerful Stealth Fighter

The F-22 zoomed onto the scene in 2005. It was the first fighter of its kind. This jet will protect the United States for years to come.

Lockheed can't sell F-22s to other countries. The U.S. government banned foreign sales.

afterburner (AF-tur-burn-uhr)—a device in the tailpipe of a turbojet engine that injects fuel into the hot gases to provide extra thrust

ban (BAN)—to forbid by law

dogfight (DAWG-fiyt)—a mid-air battle between fighter planes

drone (DROHN)—an unmanned aircraft or ship guided by remote control or onboard computer

radar (RAY-dar)—a device that sends out radio waves for finding the location and speed of a moving object

stealth (STELTH)—an aircraft design that is hard for radar to pick up

supersonic (soo-pur-SON-ik)—faster than the speed of sound; the speed of sound is about 761 miles (1,225 km) per hour.

terrorist (TER-ur-ist)—a person who uses violent acts to frighten people in order to achieve a goal

LEARN MORE

BOOKS

Garstecki, Julia. *Military Aircraft.* Military Tech. Mankato, MN: Black Rabbit Books, 2018.

Kennedy, Robert. *Would You Dare Fly a Fighter Jet?* Would You Dare? New York: Gareth Stevens, 2017.

Willis, John. *Fighter Jets.* Mighty Military Machines. New York: AV2 by Weigl, 2017.

WEBSITES

F-22 Raptor
www.af.mil/AboutUs/FactSheets/Display/tabid/224/Article/104506/f-22-raptor.aspx

F-22 Raptor
www.lockheedmartin.com/us/products/f22.html

The Most Lethal Fighter Jet in History: F-22 Raptor – Aerial Maneuvers Demo
www.youtube.com/watch?v=A4J7D9AGarE

INDEX

STADIUM

BY K.C. KELLEY

AMICUS READERS ● AMICUS INK

Amicus Readers and Amicus Ink are imprints of Amicus
P.O. Box 1329, Mankato, MN 56002
www.amicuspublishing.us

Cataloging-in-Publication Data is on file with the Library of Congress.
ISBN 978-1-68151-309-6 (library binding)
ISBN 978-1-68152-265-4 (paperback)
ISBN 978-1-68151-345-4 (eBook)

Editor: Sara Frederick
Designer: Patty Kelley
Photo Researcher/Producer: Shoreline Publishing Group LLC

Photo Credits:
Cover: Eigenswork/Wikimedia
Alamy Stock Image: DPA Picture Collection 5; Newscom: Andrew Dieb/Icon Sportswire 15; Shutterstock: Iryna Rasko 3, Poznyakov 7, Maxisport 9, feelphoto 11, Paolo Bona 12, Aspen Photo 16L, Dziurek 16T, M88 16R.

Printed in China.

HC 10 9 8 7 6 5 4 3 2 1
PB 10 9 8 7 6 5 4 3 2 1

Let's go to the soccer game!
It is played in a stadium.

SPORTING GOODS
EST1973

Ed shows his ticket.
He wears
his favorite
team's colors.

Time for a snack!
Connie has popcorn.
Matt asks
for a hot dog.

POP CORN
POP CORN

What a great view! There are a lot of people. The field is so green.

JELD-WEN
PORTLAND TIMBERS
TIMBERS 0
GALAXY 0
Alaska Airlines
CenturyLink
BURGERVILLE
adidas
fix AUTO
COLLISION
MLS FIX
D.C. UNITED
Bigfoot's
G SERIES
Allstate
Allstate
VOLKSW

What a huge screen! The score is shown there.

i-movix
extreme slow motion
HD
SprintCam

This game is on TV, too. Jess spots a camera. Smile and wave!

The game is starting. We hope our team wins!

20
10
USA

THINGS TO SEE AT A STADIUM

referees

flag

goalie